Reprogram Your Mind

An inversive way to be wealthy and successful

Ali Siddiqui

pencil

ISBN 978-93-5667-175-1
© Ali Siddiqui 2022
Published in India 2022 by Pencil

A brand of
One Point Six Technologies Pvt. Ltd.
123, Building J2, Shram Seva Premises,
Wadala Truck Terminal, Wadala (E)
Mumbai 400037, Maharashtra, INDIA
E connect@thepencilapp.com
W www.thepencilapp.com

DISCLAIMER: *The opinions expressed in this book are those of the authors and do not purport to reflect the views of the Publisher.*

Author biography

Ali Siddiqui is a blogger, tech and mindfulness enthusiast. He likes to write about habits, productivity and self-improvement. He is the author of the book "Organize your morning" and writes a monthly newsletter on substack "Organize your morning newsletter".

He is currently majoring in Computer Science and has an immense interest in working on new technologies. His curiosity always leads him to learn new things in the technology field.

For the past two years, he has been on a self-improvement journey to make his life purposeful. He always believes that if one has to be successful in life, then one needs to take small steps and focus on the process rather than the outcome.

He always believes that without commitment, we cannot start anything and without consistency, we cannot able to complete anything, so you need self-discipline in your life, not motivation.

He has written the book "Reprogram your mind" to change the mindset of young people regarding wealth and success.

CONTENTS

Introduction

About the book

Reprogram Your Mind is a self-improvement book that brings awareness to your life to achieve success. In this book, the author has used the inversive thinking method to explain how to be rich and successful which is inspired by one of Charlie Munger's speeches "How to be miserable in life".

Debunking the myth of what society tells you about getting rich and successful in life, the author explains why following and listening to people and taking their unsolicited advice, who aren't successful in life will make your life more miserable.

Who is it for?

This book is best suited for people who are just starting their new career, as well as anyone who is interested to change their mindset, getting out of the herd's mentality and to take wise decisions in their life on wealth and career.

In "Reprogram Your Mind" you'll learn:

- The consequences of listening to people who aren't successful in their life.

- Why not follow the herd in hope of being successful?

- The ways to prevent yourself from people with broke and hollow mindsets.

- An inversive method that leads you to have a growth mindset.

1. Start Tomorrow

One of the best ways to stay poor and make your life miserable is thinking to take action tomorrow instead of starting to do it today. Delaying your tasks for tomorrow not only makes you habituated to not doing things that matter and not taking action immediately but it'll make you more behind in life and makes you poor.

It's easy to fall into the trap of thinking that we'll start taking action tomorrow. We tell ourselves that we'll start eating healthy tomorrow, working out tomorrow, studying for that test tomorrow, losing weight, saving money, starting a business or learning a new skill tomorrow. But the truth is, if we don't take action today, chances are good that tomorrow will never come.

Procrastination is a habit that can be hard to break, but it's important to remember that every day we delay taking action is another day wasted. If you want to make a change in your life, there's no time like the present to start taking steps towards your goal.

Think about all the things you could accomplish if you stopped procrastinating and started taking action today. You could finally lose those extra pounds, get ahead in school or work, or even just feel better about yourself.

There's no reason to wait - so what are you waiting for? Get up and get going today!

So starting tomorrow is the best way to stay poor.

2. Read lots of books and then do nothing

Many people often talk about reading lots of books, they read so many books and they have a collection of books on their shelves to show off to others.

Reading is a good activity, but it's not enough. You need to do something with what you've learned.
What if you read a lot of books and then do nothing? Reading and doing nothing is the worst thing you can do. What's the point of reading if you don't have any actionable steps to take after reading?

If we want to get better at something, we need to take action. We need to be proactive and apply what we've learned in our real-life situations. It's not enough just by reading books and doing nothing else.

There are many people who say, "I read 52 books this year" "I have these many books" or "I have read this book and that book".

What's the use of reading so many books when you are still in the same position after reading them and not doing anything about it? So, instead of reading 52 books, read just one book and take action, and do something about it.

Reading books is a great way to learn new things, but it does not always translate into action.

Many people read a lot of books, but don't do anything with the knowledge they gained from them. This can be because the person wants to get all the information before doing anything or because he/she doesn't know how to apply what they learned.

Just because it's a book, doesn't mean you buy many books at once and you need to read all of them or read it just for reading. All the books are not meant for you.

Instead of reading many books which are recommended by someone, pick one book which is helpful for you, then learn from it and take action after reading it. Depending upon the situation and need, and what's relevant, you need to read such books.

3. Take advice from poor people on how to be rich

Think about it for a second, how foolish it would be to take advice from poor people about getting rich, it just doesn't make any sense. They don't even have any idea about it. If they had, then why are they still poor?

We listen to their baseless judgements and their opinions on why our is stupid, even though they're poor.

The reason why we should not take advice from poor people on how to be rich is that poor people are not likely to have the skills and knowledge that a rich person has. They may have been born into poverty or they may have lost their wealth due to unforeseen circumstances. So, it is difficult for them to give advice on how to become rich.

They are poor for a reason and their opinion is not worth anything.
The vast majority of people who well off have a good understanding of the value of money and they know how to handle it. They have the experience and knowledge that allows them to make sound decisions with their finances. Poor people don't have that luxury, so we should not listen to what they have to say about money or wealth.

So if you want to be poor, then take advice from poor people on how to be rich.

4. Pick a spouse who will make you feel guilty for working

This one is widespread in relationships. You have dreams to pursue but always compromise your dreams with your partner. Instead of asking for support, you are asking for permission which means you're giving them powers to control your life. They say that you shouldn't be doing this or that, and this is not good at all. Because if you don't accomplish your dreams and you did it because of them, who do you think you're going to resent? Pick a spouse that supports you even if they necessarily don't agree with you.

Some people believe that the person they marry should be their best friend, but it is also important to consider whether or not they can provide the emotional support that you need. You need someone who will understand when you are struggling with your goals and will offer advice on how to achieve them. This person should also be someone who supports your dreams and won't make you feel guilty for not living up to theirs.

It is important to choose a partner who will support you and your goals in life, not someone who will guilt you into giving up on your dreams.

The person we marry can have a profound impact on our lives. They can be our best friend, the one we share our deepest secrets with, and the one who provides us with unconditional love. But they are also the person who will make us feel guilty for following our dreams, for disagreeing with them, and for spending time away from them.

5. Fail once, quit forever

People who failed once and think it isn't for them quit forever. Failure is a part of life. It is not something that we should be ashamed of, but rather something we should learn from. People who never fail are people who never try anything new or take any risks.

Some people might think that it is better to quit and move on to something else if they fail at something, but I disagree with this idea. Quitting means giving up on your dreams and goals and settling for less than you deserve in life. Instead, we should do our best to keep working hard until we succeed rather than giving up too soon.

The most successful people in the world are those who have failed many times but never quit.

This is a quote from James Dyson, inventor of the vacuum cleaner. He is one of the most successful inventors in history and he failed many times before he came up with his invention. But he never gave up and continued to work hard until he found success.

You can be a great writer if you never give up on your work and fail a few times along the way.

Failure is a part of life, and it's important to not give up on something just because you don't see immediate results. In order to succeed in anything, you have to work hard and be willing to fail many times before you find success.

It's important to never give up when working towards a goal. Failure is part of life and the only way we learn from our mistakes is if we continue trying and don't quit.

So this is the thing that keeps people poor in their life.

6. Think that the world is fair

Another thing about being poor is to think that the world is fair. We usually complain that this is not fair, or that is not fair, but the reality is the world is always unfair, it is up to you to deal with it. All these complaints will do nothing to you. So, stop complaining about it.

The world is unfair. In fact, it is the most unfair place to live in. You might have a great life but there are people who are struggling with their lives. There are people who don't even have enough food to eat. There are people who don't have a roof over their heads. These people deserve more from the world and they deserve more from us as well.

People always complain about how unfair the world is but no one does anything about it. They say that complaining will not change anything, but if we all work together, we can make things better for everyone in this world!

The world is unfair. We've all come to that conclusion at some point in our lives. The world is unfair because of the way it treats people who are different from others. Some people get treated better than others and this is not fair, but the world doesn't care about what we think.
People can complain about the way they are treated, but this doesn't change anything. We should stop complaining and instead work hard to make a change in our own lives.

The world is unfair. It is not fair that there are people who have everything and others who have nothing. It is not fair that some people are born with a silver spoon in their mouth while others are born into poverty and crime.

We complain about the world because it seems like there is nothing we can do to change it. And, in a way, we're right - there is nothing we can do to change the world. But the world doesn't have to be unfair for us to make it better for ourselves and those around us.

7. Blame your circumstances and complain

People are always blaming their circumstances and complaining about the situations they are in. They think that if they change their situation, everything will be better. But the thing is, people need to change themselves first before anything else can happen.

The reason for this is that people tend to have a victim mentality when things go wrong. They believe that the only way to fix things is by changing their surroundings. But what people don't realize is that it's not always possible to change your surroundings, and you should never lose hope or give up on your goals because of that.

We all have our own circumstances and situations, but it is important to not blame others for them. We should stop complaining and start looking for a solution.

The word "stop" can be seen as a negative word in this context, so we can replace it with "change". This way we are not blaming or complaining about our circumstances, but instead, we are trying to find ways how to change them.

Stop blaming your circumstances and stop complaining. Instead, be grateful for what you have and work on the problem with a solution in mind. Most people don't know that they are living their best life, they are just living their life.

8. Expect the government to save you

The greatest way to stay poor is to expect the government to save you. This is the common thing people usually do especially in my country (India).

Governments are not philanthropists. They are made up of people just like you and me who want to keep their jobs and hold onto power. You cannot count on the government to save you from financial failure.

The reality is no one is going to save you except you. So, stop expecting anyone to save you during your crisis. A lot of times many people have wasted their life hoping for someone to save them and still stay poor.

9. Value the opinion of others over your own

The opinions of others are not always the best opinion. You should be able to think for yourself and not value the opinion of others over your own. It's important to have confidence in your own thoughts, ideas, and opinions.

The opinion of others can be a great thing. It can help to build relationships with people who you might not have met otherwise. But there are also times when it can be harmful, such as when someone is giving you advice about something that they know nothing about. It is important to not value the opinion of others over your own because you are the only one who knows what is best for yourself.

People often value the opinions of others over their own because they feel like they don't know enough about a topic or situation to give their own opinion. They want to avoid confrontation and so they might agree with what another person says just to keep the peace.

We should not value the opinion of others over our own. It is important to have your own opinion and stand by it. It is good to be open-minded but you should not let other people's opinions affect you too much.

People are often influenced by the opinion of others, but they should not let it affect them too much. We should have our own opinions and stand by them because it is important to be open-minded, but we shouldn't let other people's opinions affect us too much.

Success is a process, not an outcome.

10. Avoid discomfort

It is not a good idea to avoid discomfort. In fact, it is the only way to be successful and stay rich.

The key to life is accepting that discomfort will happen, and embracing it as a necessary part of life.

It's time to get uncomfortable.

If you're not uncomfortable, then you're not making progress.

Don't avoid discomfort. It is the only way to grow.

We all want to be comfortable, but in order to grow and get ahead in life, we need to face our fears and do the things that make us uncomfortable. The only way we can grow is by taking risks and stepping outside of our comfort zones.

11. Tolerate mediocrity

The greatest way to stay poor and unsuccessful in your life is to always tolerate mediocrity, settle for less and fail to reach your potential.

Stay poor, stay in a rut and find yourself in mediocrity.

Life is short, you only get one, so don't squander it by settling for things that are less important or smaller rewards than what you are truly capable of. Life holds endless possibilities and opportunities if you will only be willing and ready to seize them all. Don't tolerate mediocrity!

Don't settle for mediocrity. You are capable of so much more than you realize.

Mediocrity is a state of mind, and it's something that you can choose to avoid. The only thing that stops people from being great is themselves.

Life is short and time is fleeting, so don't be afraid to try new things in order to discover what you are capable of. Whether it's learning a new language, taking up art or becoming fluent in different fields of science, pushing yourself beyond your comfort zone can help lead you down new paths that will bring more fulfilment and happiness into your life.

Don't settle for being average, or even below average. Don't be like most people who never make any progress because they are too busy living lives of mediocrity. You have the potential to be so much more than that!

You can be the same person every day and never make any progress, or you can become someone who changes and grows as he goes along. For most people, it's better to become the former than it is to be a mediocre version of yourself.

If you tolerate the mediocrity of others, you'll get mediocrity.

If you look at successful entrepreneurs, CEOs, the best leaders, and the most successful people they hold high standards, you need to raise your standards to beat mediocrity and you should not tolerate something which is holding you back and stops your growth, so these successful people, they always keep themselves above others. The opposite of tolerance is intolerance, so you should not tolerate mediocrity at all.

So, if you want to stay poor, then tolerate mediocrity!

12. Make promises, break promises

You make promises and you break them and this is the best way to destroy your reputation which is a terrible thing to do because it takes a long time to fix it. Out of this, the hardest thing to fix is the reputation that you have with yourself, you make promises to yourself and you break promises to yourself and this is the terrible thing you can do because you're the only who is holding you accountable.

According to Alex Hormozi, *"The different version of happiness is respect for oneself."*

If you are in a habit of promising things and later breaking them, it will destroy your reputation with other people and it takes a long time to repair. If you cannot keep a promise, there is only one thing to do - don't make it!

Our society has become too accustomed to the idea of "making promises" and when you make big ones, you have to keep them. But sometimes you have to make exceptions, or bigger ones and break them. It is important, to be honest with your intentions and act accordingly.

A person who is trying to make a promise and cannot keep it should not make promises. This will only cause more trouble and damage your reputation. When you do not have the power or ability to keep a promise, it is better to say no instead of making false promises.

So you make promises to yourself and break it is the excellent way to stay poor and unsuccessful in your life.

13. Wait for perfect conditions

Don't wait for perfect conditions. A day can never be perfect, so don't wait for the perfect day and take action today.
The best way to be successful is not to let yourself get to perfect conditions. It is not about waiting for a day when everything falls into place, it is about taking action today.

By waiting for perfect conditions to make an adjustment, you will never reach your goals. Small steps, constant improvement and commitment are the key to success as well as putting in some daily practice into what works for you.

We've all seen people who spend their entire lives waiting for the perfect opportunity to get into the gym, go on vacation, or start a business. They wait by holding off until they get just the right job, each in turn. But if you delay, do you really believe that things ever go your way? The truth is that you are in control of your own life. You can make the most out of every day by taking action and making adjustments along the way.

If you want to achieve your goals, don't wait for perfect conditions or a magic moment. It will never happen. The problem is that if you wait for perfect conditions, you will never make a change.

You will always be waiting. It's like trying to lose weight by constantly dieting instead of changing your lifestyle. If you wait until you're in shape before you start working out, then it's never going to happen. The truth is that the longer you wait, the more likely it is that something will go wrong.

It may be an injury, a missed opportunity or just a bad day at work. And when it does happen, you'll wonder why you waited so long to get started. You could have been making progress toward your goals instead of wondering what could have been if only… If you wait for the perfect time, it will never come.

The only way to live a happy and successful life is to take action every day. If you don't make a move, then nothing will happen. If you want to achieve anything in life, you need to take action. The worst thing that can happen is for your dream to be put on hold because of fear or laziness.

14. Prioritize looking rich over being rich

In our society, people try to become rich by looking rich. They buy expensive things and wear fancy clothes and try to look like millionaires. But it's useless. Our society is based on an obsession with material wealth and money.

Instead of trying to look rich, learn how to become rich by putting your focus on accomplishing goals.

We all want, at some point or another in our lives, to be rich. And there's nothing wrong with that! But what do we do when we want to look like a millionaire? The answer is simple... we choose to focus on looking rich at the expense of being rich. We tend to favour material things over personal growth and happiness. This is how you can become poor faster instead of becoming rich.

The problem with looking rich is that you can't hold on to it. Sure, you may be able to show off your wealth for a while, but this will only make other people jealous and resentful. When they realize that they'll never be able to afford what you have (because it's not theirs), they will treat you badly and try to take advantage of your generosity. You don't need to be rich or have expensive things to look like a millionaire. It all starts with your mindset, and how you think about money. If you want to become rich, then focus on becoming rich instead of looking rich.

The first thing you need to do is focus on accomplishing goals instead of looking like a millionaire. If you want to become rich, stop focusing on material things and start focusing on yourself. When we look at the rich or successful people in our lives and try to emulate them, we usually focus on their physical appearance rather than their accomplishments. If you are trying to look rich, you will always be poor.

The problem with this approach is that it focuses on the wrong things. It takes your attention away from what really matters and gives it to the material things that only last for a short time before they become outdated.

So, If you want to become rich, stop focusing on material things and start focusing on yourself. When we look at the rich or successful people in our lives and try to emulate them, we usually focus on their physical appearance rather than their accomplishments. If you are trying to look rich, you will always be poor. You will never be rich unless you stop focusing on material things and start focusing on yourself. Instead of trying to look rich, focus on becoming a better person.

When we focus on our goals, we become rich. We don't need to have a lot of money to be rich. We just need to focus on what is important in our lives and not get distracted by material things. When we look at the rich or successful people in our lives and try to emulate them, we usually focus on their physical appearance rather than their accomplishments. If you are trying to look rich, you will always be poor.

Instead of focusing on what the rich or successful people in your life look like, shift your attention to what they have done. Focus on their accomplishments and how you can use those as examples for your own life.

Try to focus on the lessons you can learn from the rich and successful people in your life. Don't try to emulate their appearance, but rather what they have done with their lives. As you focus on your own achievements, you will begin to see that there is more than one way to achieve success.

You can take the path of most resistance and struggle for years only to be disappointed in how little you have accomplished or you can take a different approach and work smarter instead of harder.
You prioritize your approval more than others' opinions.

15. Avoid working on what matters most

You need to focus on what matters and let go of the unnecessary things. Most unsuccessful people avoid working on what matters, so they struggle in their life.

Working on what really matters, and letting go of the unnecessary is all that it takes to become successful
To succeed, you need to eliminate the things that aren't important and concentrate on what are. Most of us try to do too much, so we end up doing nothing well and our lives are a mess.

Successful people put all their effort into what really makes a difference.

So you need to work on what matters. Not on unnecessary things, it will not give you a higher ROI.

It's amazing what can be achieved by working on what matters and not on things that are useless. Most unsuccessful people only work on unimportant things, and so they fail in their life as well.

There are many things that we can do, but it's not important to do all of them. Successful people know what is important and what isn't. So you need to focus on what matters in life because if you don't then you will never achieve anything great.

Successful people are focused, they know what they want and how to go through it. You must be clear about your goals, and then you need to take action to achieve them. It is not easy, but it's worth trying because only by achieving goals can you become successful. So you need to work on what matters. Not on unnecessary things, it will not give you a higher ROI.

It's amazing what can be achieved by working on what matters and not on things that are useless. Most unsuccessful people only work on unimportant things, and so they fail in their life as well. If you want to be successful in life, you need to focus on what matters. Not on unimportant things, because they will not give you a higher ROI.

Many people think that working on small things is important and necessary for success, but it's not true. If you want to achieve great results in your life, then work hard only for what really matters and do not waste time on unnecessary tasks.

16. Say you're going to do something and then don't do it

Procrastination is when you don't do work but instead wait. Procrastination can be a habit, it may start small and slowly build on itself until you find yourself doing it every day without even knowing it's happening. When you have to do something but you don't do it, this is why you procrastinate because it doesn't make you feel like playing, once you drop the habit of procrastinating your work, you'll see a difference in yourself. So do the work when you have work to do!

Procrastination is a habit that you have to quit because it can lead you to be worse than you are now. So, don't procrastinate, do the work and get better results with your work.

Even if you don't feel like doing the work, whether it be cleaning up your room, studying for a test or writing an essay, you must do it and find ways to motivate yourself to get it done.

When you procrastinate, you give yourself extra excuses and more opportunities to delay doing what needs to be done.

Procrastination is a habit that can be broken with the right combination of willpower and motivation. Procrastination comes from an inability to make decisions and this habit does not allow you to see the bigger picture. You need to manage your time better and understand what it takes for you to complete every task which includes knowing your own limitations as well.

Procrastination can lead to feelings of stress and anxiety. This is because you are putting off important tasks that need to be done, but instead of doing them, you find yourself doing other things that may seem more interesting at the moment. When this happens, it can cause problems in your personal relationships as well as at work.

Procrastination can be a habit that is hard to break. It often starts as an innocent way to avoid doing something that you are not prepared for or don't want to do. You begin by putting things off, but before you know it, it becomes a habit and you find yourself doing it more often.

17. Do what everyone else is doing

Most people fail in life because they don't use their minds in the correct way, instead, they follow others blindly to be on the safer side to avoid failure or at least to fear failure.

You don't have to do what everyone else is doing. If you find something that works for you and your business, stick with it. Don't switch up your routine every time something different comes along.

Never do what everyone else is doing. Do what you're inspired to do even if it seems like a risk. You can't control outcomes, but you can always control how you act and how hard you work.

There is no secret formula to success. Every successful person has gone through a process of trial and error to find their niche and figure out how to be successful. It may feel like there is more pressure on you than ever before, but the truth is that it's normal for everyone to get doubts about themselves once in a while.

Don't let the pressures of life get you down. Things will be okay, and even if they are not, there is always a way to make them better. You just have to keep moving forward. The key is to not let the doubts control you. This is the only way you will be able to achieve your goals and live the life that you deserve.

It's important to remember that you are not alone, and there is no secret formula for success.

The only thing that matters is doing the work and being consistent. You will get through this because you have a strong support system around you.

If you want to be successful, you have to take risks and put yourself out there. You can't let fear hold you back. It's also normal to feel like you aren't good enough or that you can't do anything right.

It's hard not to compare yourself to others and think about how they do things better than you do. But the reality is that no one is perfect, and comparing yourself to others will only make you feel worse about yourself.

18. Do your best, not what it takes

Your best self sucks!

Life is too short and precious to waste time on watery thoughts and emotions. No one cares that you've given your best and you didn't succeed in what you want to achieve. You need to be better and do what's required. If you are incapable of doing something, then be better and your best will surpass what it requires.

No one cares if you did your best or not. What matters is that you did something and gave it your all.

Your best isn't good enough, your best needs to be better. Do what it takes for you to achieve your goals without feeling that any of your efforts are wasted.

If your best isn't good enough, then you need to do something about it. You need to be better or at least try harder than before. Your best is only good when it's the result of hard work and dedication. You have to do what's required of you, no matter how much it hurts.

You need to be better than the rest and give it your all. If you are incapable of doing something, then be better and your best will surpass what it requires.

You will never get what you want if you don't try your best. If you are incapable of doing something, then be better and your best will surpass what it requires.

You have to try your best for what it takes by being better than before. Your best isn't good enough, your best needs to be better.

If you're not feeling confident and inspired, then it's time to do your best. Be proud of yourself as you are capable of something amazing. Never give up, keep going and let your best do the talking!

19. Talk more, do less

Successful people are focused on their work, not on talking. They know that time is limited and there are so many things they should be doing that wasting it in unnecessary conversations isn't worth it.

Many successful people know that they need less talking and more doing. The most successful people in any field have a tremendous ability to focus on what's important, and not waste time on unessential things like social media and text messages.

Stop wasting your time with unnecessary chitchat. Focus on the job at hand, put in the real effort and get more satisfactory results.

The world has changed a lot since the birth of our universe. Making your work and life easier wouldn't be something new to most people, but it is not enough to just make everything easier. Your focus should be on doing more than talking about doing less.

The world is getting more complex, and it's only going to get worse. Your focus should be on doing more than talking about doing less. The most successful people in any field have a tremendous ability to focus on what's important, and not waste time on unessential things like social media and text messages. Stop wasting your time with unnecessary chitchat. Focus on the job at hand, put in the real effort and get more satisfactory results.

The secret to success is simple: focus on what's important, not unimportant things.

The key is not to waste time, so you can be more productive and effective in everything that you do. The best way to get better results is by focusing on the work at hand. Stop wasting time with unnecessary chitchat. Focus on the job at hand and put in the real effort.

20. Start something new today, start something new tomorrow

People get bored very easily and they start a new project. It's OK to get stuck, but don't just leave it incomplete and start another new thing. Come on people, complete one task at a time or take some time off to think about what should be done next.

Today is the day to complete your first task. Don't start something new. If you do, you'll never find the time to finish it. By starting a single task and completing it, you'll learn how to manage a project and people, both of which come with their own challenges.

What's the most common mistake that people make when starting something new? They say "Is this a good idea or not?" and then start. The moment they get bored or feel insecure, they stop. They don't complete anything; they are never happy until they find a new alternative to do things with.

Start the new year out on a good note by completing your first task. Everyone has heard of starting something new that you're excited about, but most people find themselves getting bored and abandoning the project after spending a few hours or even days working on it. Start today, and complete a small portion today to keep you motivated for the completion of your first real challenge for the day!

If you're bored, I challenge you to complete at least one task that you have been putting off. You can start by making a list of all the things that need to get done, and then working on them one at a time. When you start a new project or goal, it's important to have a plan for how you're going to complete it.

In the beginning stages of your project, focus on small wins by focusing on completing one task at a time. The more tasks that you complete, the closer you get to finishing your project! If you're feeling stuck, try to break the project down into smaller chunks that are easier to accomplish. If you don't know what to do first, write out a list of tasks that need to be done and start at the top.

Keep track of your progress by writing down what you have completed each day or week. The first step to start is to simply start, and you will be amazed at how much more you can accomplish when you don't waste time procrastinating. The moment they get bored or feel insecure, they stop. They don't complete anything; they are never happy until they find a new alternative to do things with.

21. Believe what other people think about you more than what you think about you

What you believe about yourself has a more significant impact than what others think about you. We are more passionate, vain and distracted by the opinions of others than we are by our own thoughts. But how do you know how you really feel? Especially if your self-esteem is low, it might be challenging to tell the difference between what others say and what is true for you.

A key to growing self-esteem is being able to distinguish between what others say and what you believe. This may take some practice but it's well worth the effort. Why? Because when you can separate the two, you have more control over your life.

There are two ways to find out what you really think about yourself. The first is through self-reflection. This means taking time to explore your thoughts, feelings and emotions. You can do this through journaling, meditation or talking with a friend who listens well. The second way is by asking for feedback from others in situations where they have no reason to lie or sugarcoat the truth.

Most people live their lives around what other people think about them, yet don't give a damn about what they feel about themselves. It is not uncommon for people to feel like they are in a rut. They don't feel motivated, inspired or excited about anything. They may have lost their passion and desire for life.

The answer to this problem isn't more self-help books, motivational speakers or workshops; it is within you. This is a dangerous way of living because it means you are always trying to please others and live up to their expectations. It's exhausting and doesn't allow you to be yourself. Because of this, we can often get lost in a world that is not our own.

We are so focused on what others think of us that we forget who we are and what makes us unique. If you allow other people to define your self-worth, then you will never be satisfied with yourself because they always have something more to say.

It's not surprising that some people spend their lives trying to please others, or avoid making a fool of themselves. They have low self-esteem and don't believe they are worthy of being loved or accepted by others. Their thoughts are often negative and they feel powerless over their lives because they don't realize that their own thoughts create the world around them.

22. Make a mistake then wait and repeat

One of the easiest ways to stop your growth is to make mistakes but not learn and improve from them, instead repeating those mistakes constantly. The only way you can change this is by getting feedback from your mentors, coaches and peers, who are there to help you learn from your mistakes.

Mistakes are part of the process. Your business is never one-size-fits-all, so don't try to fit it into a cookie-cutter model. Learn from your mistakes and build on them to become a better business owner.

Our learning process is designed to never repeat a mistake. We make mistakes in order to learn how to improve on them and fix them the next time. It may seem slightly impossible at first but let's try it and see how things go.

It is vital to learn from mistakes, not just from successes. If you keep making the same mistakes over and over again, you'll never grow as a person.

You'll never be able to help others, and you won't be able to reach your full potential. If you're looking for a way to make a difference in the world, start by learning from your mistakes and making them into something positive. This is why we are always striving to learn from our mistakes so that we can fix them.

Instead of trying to avoid making mistakes, focus on learning from them. Once you have learned what not to do, you can prevent yourself from making the same mistake again in the future. This is how people grow as individuals and businesses grow with them.

In order to grow and succeed, you need to know what not to do. If you have made a mistake in the past, don't try to forget about it or sweep it under the rug. Instead, focus on learning from your mistakes so that they don't happen again. This is one of the keys to success in any industry: learning from others' mistakes and applying them to your own life.

If you want to be successful, you need to learn from your mistakes. The sooner you can identify and fix your mistakes, the better off you will be in the long run. This is why we are always striving to learn from our mistakes so that we can fix them. If you don't learn from your mistakes, you will never be able to improve yourself or the world around you.

By being open to change and learning from your mistakes, you can make positive changes in your life and build a better future for everyone around you. When you make a mistake, don't be afraid to admit it. You will have a much easier time learning from your mistakes if you can see them for what they are: opportunities to grow and improve. Don't try to hide from them or pretend that they never happened; instead, look at them head-on.

23. Be Replaceable

If you want to get ahead in your career, then you need to be irreplaceable. Do such things that 99% of people aren't good enough doing such things, or do it if it's uncommon. Create your own niche. Be different and stand out.

The world is full of people who do things because everyone else does them. If you want to stand out, then don't be one of those people. Instead, be different and do things that no one else does. Don't be like everyone else. Be an individual. Be original, if possible. No one will remember you if they see that you are like everyone else in the world. This will give you a competitive advantage.

The point is, don't settle for the common practices of your industry. If people aren't doing it well already and your role requires such things, then why not do them better, or more uncommonly?

If you're anything less than unique, then, in today's topsy-turvy job market, you're toast. Our world is changing too fast for any one person to be able to do it all. You need to learn how to focus and prioritize and hire people who can do what you do best.

You must differentiate yourself from the rest of the crowd.

You have to stand out. You must be the best in your field, or better yet, the only one who does what you do. You need to stand out. You must be the best at something and make sure it's what people want most in your industry. You should be able to focus on the things that only you can do. And then, when you need more help, hire someone who does what you don't.

Don't ever let yourself become a jack of all trades and master of none. The best way to differentiate yourself is by being different. You can't just be like everyone else and expect anyone to notice you. They won't. If they do, they'll quickly forget what they saw because there's so much competition out there today that it's easy for people to get lost in the shuffle.

24. Do what everyone else is doing, do it for less

You cannot get ahead in your life if you constantly do something that everyone else is doing and do it for less. A practical, bold and courageous approach to business strategy is required by any vessel crossing the sea of opportunity.

The only way to be truly successful is to adopt a bold, practical, and courageous approach to business strategy. Most people settle for doing something that everyone else is doing and doing it for less.

A strong, consistent and effective strategic plan is necessary to achieve any goals in business.

Any product that everybody else is doing is a product nobody needs. Products should solve problems and have special value beyond the norm. The strategy of attacking an existing market with a lower price and higher volume product is as limited as taking the most direct route across the ocean.

Strange as it may appear, some people think they can get ahead by doing the same things others are doing...isn't it funny?

Be the best in your industry. But before you begin to stand out, note one important distinction. The difference is not in how you do things as much as what.

Have you ever been to a fast food restaurant that has no drive-thru? Have you ever driven at night without your headlights? Do your coworkers take the stairs to their offices?

People will only remember you if they believe in you and believe that you are doing something that those around them are not. If the other option is to be branded as someone who does things for less, then you will be going down the wrong path. Stake your claim in the world and do what everyone else is not doing, do it for more.

The way to success is through hard work. If you're not willing to do what everyone else is doing and if you do it for less and compare it with others, then you won't be able to rise above mediocrity. You will have your weaknesses and shortcomings, but you have to always look forward in your life.

As much as I may want to achieve success by only doing what everyone else is doing, it is not the right way to go. I have a feeling that everyone else is doing something for less than what you are getting for yourself, maybe even twice as much.

It is important to find what you want to do and do it better than anyone else. If you don't have a goal, then you'll never be able to achieve anything in life. You will have your weaknesses and shortcomings, but you have to always look forward in your life.

As much as I may want to achieve success by only doing what everyone else is doing, it is not the right way to go. You can't just sit there and wait for things to happen, you have to take action. You need to put yourself in the right place at the right time and then do what everyone else is not doing.

If you want success in life, it will come if you work hard enough for it. That's why you have to be willing to do what everyone else is not doing. You have to get up and go out of your comfort zone and do something that will make you stand out from the rest. If you can't do that, then you won't be able to rise above mediocrity. Being a successful person is not just about how much money you make, it's also about how you go about making that money. If you want to be successful, then you have to learn how to do things differently than everyone else.

25. Find something that works and then stop doing it.

If you pick something interesting to do, then complete it right away, don't leave it incomplete, you'll never be able to complete it if you always stop doing such things after starting. You need to keep moving forward and not give up after failing a few times because the best way to keep improving is by failing all the time.

Before you start, take a few moments to think about why you really want to start. Figure out something that suits your personality and helps your life. Don't pick something that seems interesting at first, but you never complete it or it's hard to complete. Picking easy and useful things to do will increase your chance of succeeding. If you never give up after starting and keep pushing forward, gradually you'll find an enjoyable thing that keeps improving.

You need to start the learning process sooner rather than later because you need to have constant corrections in your performance based on the outcome. You need to improve every day and not wait for tomorrow, failure will occur if you stop trying after an unsuccessful attempt. It's important to get feedback and be self-aware.

If you want to be good at something, do it every day. You have to love it, though. You have to practice every single day and never give up. You will get a lot better as long as you work hard, but if you're not passionate about it then you won't get anywhere.

As we all know, the best way to learn is to try and keep trying. If you create a game plan and accomplish it each day, you'll reach your goal so much faster.

Never giving up is what sets great entrepreneurs apart from the average person. It takes emotional intelligence, discipline and resilience to follow through every day on your goals, whether you achieve them or not.

Complete the task before leaving it, you'll never be able to finish it if you don't always complete your task once started.

Why would you leave it incomplete? It is better to start something and complete it than never do it at all.

If you find something fun to do, then do it now! Don't let it be a waste of time. Life is too short, so do things that make you happy and that brighten your life.

Don't let the fear of failure stop you from doing things. You can't live your life in fear of what other people think of you or what might happen if you fail. If you're not doing something because you're afraid of failing, then that's a waste.

Don't procrastinate, as it is a waste of time. Don't put things off until tomorrow; do them today! You will never be able to finish what you started if you keep putting it off all the time. Always try to be the best, and don't give up after failing.

The only way to succeed is by trying and trying again until you finally get it right. If you keep doing what you're doing now, then nothing will change because that's how things are right now. It doesn't matter how hard it is or what other people say about your plans, just do it!

26. Hire dumb people

In fact, hiring dumb people for your team will only make things worse. Let alone their performance, you can't even predict what would be the next thing to hit them. Always choose someone who has proven performance and experience in this kind of situation.

If a candidate didn't get the job because he was dumb, it would be good for your company. If a candidate is dumb but got what he wanted, it wouldn't benefit you. If a candidate is right for your company, that's great. But hiring dumb people will never benefit anyone except dumb people—and that's not who we are at all.

If you're going to hire people, you must understand that it's a two-sided relationship. Smart person will learn from their mistakes but also learns from the company's mistake. You can't just hire and forget about them.

If you hire smart people, they will help you grow. If you hire dumb people, they will drag your company down.

The bottom line is this: if someone is an idiot and gets what he wants—he's not going to be a good employee. He'll just cheat the system by being dumb but getting what he wants out of it. It's important to keep in mind that people aren't just tools for you to use. They aren't objects or robots.

People have feelings, emotions, and lives outside of the workplace. If you treat them as such, they will appreciate it and work harder for you. Smart people are also faster learners than average ones because they tend to understand concepts faster (and more easily) than others do.

Smart people do better at their jobs. They take more initiative, they don't make dumb mistakes, and they're generally just a lot more productive than someone who's not very smart. If you have several employees who are all smart but one is especially bright, then the company will be better off with that one person than without him or her.

You have to be there for them. You have to give them the tools they need and help them out when they're struggling. If we hire people that are not as smart as us, it means that we will have to work harder than them. This doesn't mean you should hire only the most qualified candidates—far from it!

27. Assume you are always right

It is important to remember that assuming you are always right will never make you successful in life. The truth is that one's views on the world depend on the situation and one should be flexible enough to accept other people's ideas and opinions.

When it comes to taking decisions, always try to let go of your ego. You need to learn how to argue your point of view in a civil manner. You should also remember that you cannot do everything on your own and should ask others' opinions while making a decision.

No one can be right all the time, and you will never win an argument if you are unwilling to listen to what others have to say. Always consider other people's views before making a decision.

I believe it is important to be open to others' perspectives because it makes the world a better place and makes people want to interact.

It's good to have opinions and to have an independent viewpoint, but that doesn't give you a license to apply them to everything. There are many things in life you should not be so rigid about.

While you know that you are right, remember that if you can't convince and lead other people, your opinion is worthless. Convincing others is an art and attitude for a true leader.

Consider the possibility that you may be wrong.

If you think that you are always right, then you will never be successful in life. You will be too stubborn to make any changes or take any risks. For example, if your boss is trying to motivate you or correct your mistakes, it could make you defensive and defensive.

Success does not come from your grandiose ideas, but from the small daily steps, you make. Your goal is not to make yourself feel better about yourself, but to let go of expectations from others and from yourself.

When you assume the best in others, you will get the best out of them. If you'd rather be liked by everyone than respected by some, or if you believe your opinions should be given greater weight than those of others, it is important to understand that this is not a sign of strength.

28. Make money. Spend more than you make

The last thing to stay poor and miserable in your life is to spend more

Keeping expenses lower than what you earn is a good way to save. It doesn't make sense to spend more than you make on things that don't bring value to our lives.

Keeping your expenditure lower than what you earn is an important part of financial freedom. If you keep it low, you can be financially secure without spending any extra money.

The best way to improve your financial situation is to make money the old-fashioned way: Save it! And make sure you don't spend more than you earn. Here are my tips for remaining frugal.

This is how you keep control of your finances and make sure that you're only spending what you're making.

Being free of financial stress isn't a far-off fantasy. You just need to go through the right steps. By keeping your spending low and your income high, you can be financially secure without breaking a sweat.

When you spend less than you earn, that surplus money can help you achieve financial freedom.

The need to keep spending low is very important in the journey to financial security. The key to this is having a solid budget. A good budget is essential for building assets, but you also shouldn't forget about its basic functions, which are spending and saving.

You dream of being financially secure, but it's hard to do when you're spending all your money. Most people find themselves in a constant loop of working more just to keep up with bills.

No matter how easily you make money, times always change. It's just a part of life. The reason why we recommend you save enough is that you never know what kind of issue might come up in the future.

Wrap up

You are now at the end of the book. I hope you've learnt something from this book. Now apply all these rules in your life, and you'll notice that your brain tends to attract and process negative things faster than positive things, so use this trick if you want to upgrade your mindset. This type of thinking is called "Inversion Thinking".

So what exactly is inversion thinking?

Inversion is thinking of what you want to achieve in reverse. Another way to put it is instead of thinking about the future results, and what you want to achieve, you think to flip it in reverse and think about what you don't want to happen.

For example, If you want a happy relationship, ask yourself how to ruin a relationship. You'll now get several ways to ruin a relationship, so you'll avoid it.

By this, you'll get an idea of what you don't want to happen in life, so willingly, you'll avoid it because now you learned the consequences of what happens if you do the flip side of something that you need.

Use the inversion thinking method to question yourself and solve your problems faster and take wise decisions in your life.

Inversion thinking is a skill that we learn in life; typically, this type of thinking is not approached in school-based learning. It is a subject that I stumbled across as I read more about Charlie Munger and listened to his speeches.

Use Inversion thinking to get what you want in your life.

As you've completed reading this entire book, here's a quick recap of what you've learned now in the actual form:

1. **Start today!**
2. **Read books and do the stuff in the books**
3. **Take advice from rich people on how to be rich**
4. **Pick a spouse who makes you feel awesome about working**
5. **Fail once, try again**
6. **Think the world is unfair and act accordingly**
7. **Never blame your circumstances, thank your circumstances for making you who you are**

8. **Instead of complaining, do something**
9. **Expect no one to save you except for yourself**
10. **Value your opinion over other those of other people**
11. **Seek out discomfort**
12. **Tolerate nothing but excellence**
13. **Make promises, keep promises**
14. **Wait for the worst conditions, wait for imperfect conditions and act anyways on what you want**
15. **Avoid working on the stuff that doesn't matter, work on the things that matter most, and ignore the rest**
16. **Say you are going to do something and then do it**
17. **Do what no one else is doing**

18. **Do your best and make it above what it takes to be successful**
19. **Talk less, do more**
20. **Start something new today and keep at it, until you are good to do it so long that it would be unreasonable for you to be bad**
21. **Don't believe what other people think about you more than what you think yourself**
22. **Be irreplaceable**
23. **Find something that works and don't stop doing it.**
24. **Keep doing it until you are bored out of your mind because you are so good at doing that thing that works**
25. **Hire smart people**
26. **Assume you are always wrong**
27. **Be willing to learn**
28. **Make money and spend less than you make**

Charlie Munger and His Impact on Inversion Thinking

"Invert, always invert: Turn a situation or problem upside down. Look at it backwards. What happens if all our plans go wrong? Where don't we want to go, and how do you get there? Instead of looking for success, make a list of how to fail instead – through sloth, envy, resentment, self-pity, entitlement, and all the mental habits of self-defeat. Avoid these qualities and you will succeed. Tell me where I'm going to die, that is, so I don't go there."

www.ingramcontent.com/pod-product-compliance
Lightning Source LLC
LaVergne TN
LVHW041747190726
843493LV00008B/2488